Angel Falls, South America

Publisher: Melissa Fairley
Art Director: Faith Booker
Editor: Victoria Garrard
Designer: Emma Randall
Production Controller: Ed Green
Production Manager: Suzy Kelly

ISBN: 978 1 84898 208 6

Printed in China
1 3 5 7 9 10 8 6 4 2

Picture credits (t=top; b=bottom; c=centre; l=left; r=right; OFC=outside front cover):
Bethel Area Chamber of Commerce: 16–17, 28bl. Bettmann/Corbis: 4. Bryan Berg, Cardstacker: 26, 27, 28tr.
Carol Savage Photography: OFC. Courtesy of Six Flags Great Adventure: 8, 9, 29tl. Ken Fisher/Getty Images: 21.
Getty Images: 6–7, 28tl. iStock: 1, 5 both, 19bl, 20, 22bA, 23bB, 24, 25, 29cr, 29bl. National Geographic/Getty Images:
15. Shutterstock: 2, 10b, 10–11, 12–13, 14–15, 18, 19br, 22bB, 22bC, 22bD, 22bE, 23bA, 23bC, 23bD, 23bE, 28br,
29tr, 29cl, 29br, 31. Steve Sillett: 19t.

Thank you to Lorraine Petersen and the members of nasen

Every effort has been made to trace copyright holders, and we apologize in advance for any omissions.
We would be pleased to insert the appropriate acknowledgements in any subsequent edition of this publication.

NOTE TO READERS
The website addresses are correct at the time of publishing. However, due to the ever-changing
nature of the internet, websites and content may change. Some websites can contain links that
are unsuitable for children. The publisher is not responsible for changes in content or website
addresses. We advise that internet searches should be supervised by an adult.

CONTENTS

Mount Everest, Asia

INTRODUCTION

This book is all about the world's tallest things.

From tall people...

...to tall buildings...

...to the tallest mountain on Earth.

Robert Wadlow is
the tallest person
in recorded history.
He was 2.72 metres tall.

The Burj Dubai in the United Arab Emirates is nearly a kilometre high!

Climbing Mount Everest can be very dangerous. Between 1921 and 2006 the mountain claimed a total of 212 lives.

TALLEST MAN

The world's tallest living man is named Sultan Kosen. He is the Guinness World Record holder.

Sultan is 2.465 metres tall.

Sultan's hands measure 27.5 centimetres.

Sultan lives in Turkey. He became the Guinness World Record holder in 2009. He has visited London and New York to appear on TV.

"The most difficult things are I can't fit into a normal car. I can't go shopping like normal people. I have to have things made specially. The good thing about being so tall is at home they use my height to change the light bulbs and hang the curtains, things like that."
Sultan Kosen

Sultan's feet measure 36.5 centimetres.

TALLEST ROLLERCOASTER

The riders count down...

five,
four,
three,
two,
one!

Kingda Ka is 139 metres tall.

You zoom from 0 to 206 kilometres per hour in just 3.5 seconds.

You climb up and up until you are 45 storeys high!

Then you drop down and down.

It's 59 seconds of terror.

It's Kingda Ka – the world's tallest rollercoaster.

Kingda Ka is in New Jersey, USA.

TALLEST BRIDGE

The Millau Viaduct in France is the world's tallest bridge.

Its tallest point is 343 metres high. That's taller than the Eiffel Tower in Paris, France!

324m

Eiffel Tower

343m

Millau Viaduct

Millions of cars drive over the bridge every year. This puts lots of stress on the bridge. There are sensors on the bridge to measure the stress.

Pier 2 is the tallest pier. It is 245 metres high.

Pylon

Pier

TALLEST ICEBERG

An iceberg is a giant chunk of floating ice.

The tallest iceberg ever recorded was spotted in the Atlantic Ocean.

The iceberg measured 168 metres. That's the height of a really tall skyscraper!

168 metres

That was its height above sea level. However, most of an iceberg is under the water.

No one knows how big the whole iceberg was!

Sea level

13

TALLEST MOUNTAIN

The tallest mountain in the world is Mount Everest. It is in Asia.

Mount Everest is 8,850 metres high. The height of a mountain is measured from sea level to its summit.

Summit

Mount Everest

To reach the summit, climbers must enter the "Death Zone".

This is the part of a mountain above 7,000 metres. There is not enough oxygen at this height.

Lack of oxygen can make climbers ill. Sometimes they can even die. Most climbers breathe oxygen from tanks.

Oxygen mask

Oxygen tank

TALLEST SNOWWOMAN

For nine years, the world's tallest snowman was "Angus, King of the Mountain".

Angus was built by the people of Bethel, in Maine, USA. He was 34.6 metres tall.

Then, in 2008, Angus lost his record!

The people of Bethel built a new giant – Olympia SnowWoman!

She was 37.2 metres tall. It took over 100 people to build the record-breaking snowwoman.

They used 5.8 million kilograms of snow.

Tree arms

Olympia SnowWoman

Eyelashes made from skis

Tyres (for the mouth and buttons)

TALLEST TREE

The tallest tree on Earth is a sequoia, or redwood tree. It is growing in California, USA.

Redwood tree

Scientists think the tree could be 800 years old. It was found by a scientist named Steve Sillett. Steve climbs the world's tallest trees. He studies the trees and measures them.

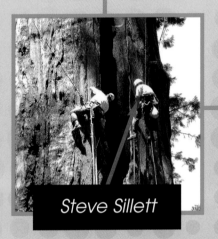

Steve Sillett

Steve climbed to the top of the tallest tree. He dropped a tape measure from the top of the tree down to the ground. It measured 115.57 metres!

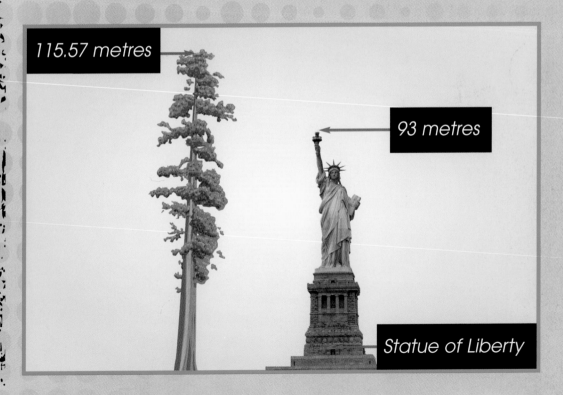

115.57 metres

93 metres

Statue of Liberty

TALLEST WATERFALL

The tallest waterfall in the world is Angel Falls. It is in Venezuela in South America and is **979** metres high.

Angel Falls

Some people want to get a close-up look at the waterfall. They BASE jump from the top of Angel Falls!

A BASE jumper jumps from a fixed object. The jumper freefalls for a few seconds before opening their parachute.

BASE jumper in freefall

TOP TEN TALLEST MAN-MADE STRUCTURES

Here are the top ten tallest structures in the world. How much taller can we go?

Greenland Square Zifeng Tower
Nanjing, China
450 metres

John Hancock Center
Chicago, USA
457 metres

Shanghai World Financial Center
Shanghai, China
492 metres

Petronas Tower 1 and 2
Kuala Lumpur, Malaysia
452 metres

Oriental Pearl Tower
Shanghai, China
468 metres

Taipei 101
Taipei, Taiwan
508 metres

Ostankino Tower
Moscow, Russia
540 metres

Burj Dubai
Dubai, United Arab Emirates
818 metres

Willis Tower
Chicago, USA
527 metres

CN Tower
Toronto, Canada
553 metres

TALLEST MAN-MADE STRUCTURE

The Burj Dubai is the world's tallest building and man-made structure. It is 818 metres tall.

The Burj Dubai

The Burj Dubai is in the United Arab Emirates.
The word "burj" means tower in Arabic.

Inside the tower there are offices and apartments.
There is an outdoor swimming pool on the 78th floor.
There is also a hotel designed by Georgio Armani.

The tower's lifts have to travel fast!

The fastest lift travels at around ten metres per second.

TALLEST HOUSE OF CARDS

Bryan Berg is a record-breaking cardstacker. In 2007, Bryan built the world's tallest house of cards.

The building is 7.85 metres high.
Bryan used 57,240 cards.

Bryan does not use glue or tape.

His secret is to stack the cards in grids.

This makes the buildings strong.

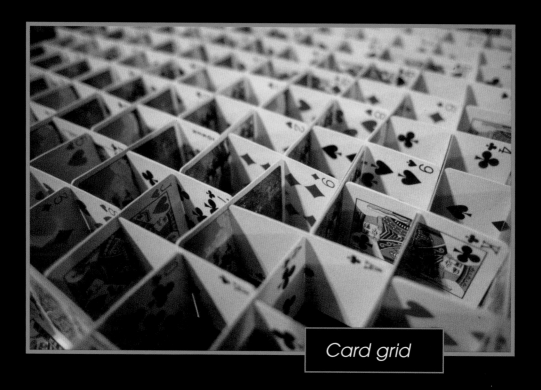

Card grid

Bryan Berg and his house of cards.

TOP TEN TALLEST

Some of the tallest things on Earth were created by nature.

Others were built by humans.

They are all amazing record breakers.

10

Tallest man:

Sultan Kosen, 2.465 metres

9

Tallest house of cards:

Bryan Berg's, 7.85 metres

8

Tallest snowwoman:

Olympia, 37.2 metres

7

Tallest tree:

Redwood in California,
115.57 metres

6

Tallest rollercoaster:

Kingda Ka, 139 metres

5

Tallest iceberg:

168 metres

4

Tallest bridge:

Millau Viaduct, 343 metres

3

Tallest building:

Burj Dubai, 818 metres

2

Tallest waterfall:

Angel Falls, 979 metres

1

Tallest mountain:

Mount Everest, 8,850 metres

NEED TO KNOW WORDS

Arabic A language spoken in countries such as the United Arab Emirates, Egypt and Iraq.

BASE jump A parachute jump made from a fixed object, such as a high building, instead of from a plane.

freefall In skydiving, this is the part of the jump before the parachute opens.

Guinness World Records An organization that records and measures record-breaking things and events. The world records are then published in a book each year.

man-made Created or constructed by humans.

oxygen A gas that humans, animals and plants need in order to live.

sea level The surface of the sea. It is used as a starting point for measuring the height of land and mountains.

sensor A piece of equipment that can sense things such as movement, sound, heat, light or pressure.

skyscraper A very tall building that tends to dominate a skyline.

storey One level, or floor, in a building.

stress When talking about structures, this word means the forces and pressure on a structure which may cause it to wear away or break.

structure Something that has been constructed such as a building, tower, statue or bridge.

summit The highest point, or top, of something.

TALL FACTS

- Mauna Kea is an inactive volcano. It forms part of the island of Hawaii. Mauna Kea is just over 10,200 metres tall. Why isn't it the tallest mountain on Earth? That's because mountains are measured from sea level. Only the top 4,205 metres of Mauna Kea are above sea level.

- The Royal Gorge Bridge in Colorado, USA, is suspended (hung) between two giant cliffs. This means it isn't a tall bridge, but it is the world's highest bridge. From the platform to the river below is a drop of 321 metres.

Platform

Cliff

FIND OUT MORE ONLINE...

www.altonweb.com/history/wadlow/

www.burjdubaiskyscraper.com/

www.bethelmainesnowwoman.com/index.html

www.leviaducdemillau.com/english/divers/gallerie.html

INDEX